AF432627

THE ONLY BOOK YOU NEED TO START YOUR PODCAST

The complete guide

Why Podcasting? - The boom

You've heard it before: everybody has a podcast. Your cousin has a podcast, that guy from your high school reunion? Yeah, he's got one too. Even your mom's book club is considering starting a podcast (spoiler: it's going to be all about Jane Austen). So here you are, reading the introduction of yet another book that promises to tell you how to start your own podcast, and you're thinking, Do I really need to join the podcast bandwagon? The short answer? Yes. Yes, you do. But before we dive headfirst into the podcasting pool, let's take a moment to look around. Podcasting is not just a passing fad or some fleeting trend. It's not like fidget spinners or 3D movies. Podcasting is the real deal. In fact, it's been growing steadily since the early 2000s, and there's no sign of it slowing down. But what is it about podcasting that makes it so irresistible?

Let's start with some numbers, shall we? (Don't worry, I promise they'll be interesting.) According to recent data, more than half of all Americans over the age of 12 have listened to a podcast at some point in their lives. That's around 144 million people. And every week, more than 60 million people tune in to their favorite shows. Globally, that number is even higher, with podcasting audiences growing in countries like the UK, Australia, and Brazil. Podcasting is an international phenomenon.

Still not convinced? Let's think about the possibilities. Podcasting is one of the most accessible forms of media today. You don't need a broadcasting degree, a fancy studio, or a team of producers to get started. You don't even need to put on pants! (Though it is recommended if you're recording with a co-host. Trust me, it's just polite.) All you really need is a microphone, an internet connection, and something to say. The barriers to entry are lower than ever, making it possible for anyone—yes, even you—to create and distribute content to a potentially massive audience.

The beauty of podcasting is that it's intimate. It's not like scrolling through a social media feed or watching a video on YouTube. Podcasts have this strange and wonderful ability to make listeners feel like they're part of a conversation, even if they're just passively listening while washing dishes or stuck in traffic. Your voice is literally in their ears. Think about that for a second: podcasting allows you to whisper your message directly into the ears of thousands (or millions!) of people. That's some powerful stuff.

Why Podcasting is More Than a Trend

Let's take a step back and look at why podcasting has endured—and why it's not going anywhere anytime soon. First and foremost, it's because of how easily podcasts fit into our daily lives. Podcasts can be consumed while you're doing other things. You can listen while commuting, cleaning, working out, or even trying to fall asleep. Try doing that with a blog post or a video series.

Unlike video content, which demands your full attention, podcasts are the perfect multitasking medium. You don't have to sit in front of a screen or scroll through pages of text. You just pop in your earbuds and go. The flexibility podcasts offer is a major reason they've become so popular. Listeners can consume your content wherever and whenever they want.

Another reason podcasting has staying power is the sheer variety of content. Whether you're into crime stories, self-help, history, cooking, video games, or conspiracy theories about ancient aliens building the pyramids (hey, no judgment), there's a podcast out there for you. And if there's not? Guess what—that's an opportunity for *you* to fill that gap! People are looking for niche content, and podcasts allow creators to dive deep into those subjects in ways that other media can't.

The third and perhaps most important reason podcasting isn't just a passing trend is the sense of connection it fosters between the host and the audience. There's something uniquely intimate about hearing someone's voice on a regular basis. Over time, listeners start to feel like they know the host, even if they've never met. This bond is what turns casual listeners into devoted fans. A podcast can become part of someone's weekly routine—like catching up with a friend over coffee, except the coffee is optional, and you're probably talking to yourself into a microphone. But hey, that's part of the magic.

Podcasting for Passion and Profit

Now, before you get too carried away thinking this book is going to make you an instant podcasting millionaire, let's have a little heart-to-heart. Podcasting can absolutely open doors to opportunities—financial and otherwise. Some podcasts make serious bank through sponsorships, ads, and listener support on platforms like Patreon. However, for the vast majority of podcasters, the real reward isn't monetary (though making some extra cash certainly doesn't hurt). It's about sharing something you love with an audience that appreciates it.

Many successful podcasts started as passion projects, and the money (if it came at all) followed later. That's not to say you can't monetize your podcast, because you absolutely can. But if your main motivation for podcasting is to "get rich quick," you might be setting yourself up for disappointment.

Like most creative endeavours, success in podcasting takes time, effort, and persistence.

What's more important is finding a topic you're passionate about—something you'd enjoy talking about, even if no one were listening. That enthusiasm will translate into your recordings, and listeners will pick up on it. People are drawn to authenticity. They want to hear someone who's genuinely excited about the subject they're discussing, not someone who's phoning it in for a paycheck.

That's not to say you can't have ambitious goals for your podcast. You should! This book will help you dream big while keeping your expectations grounded in reality. We'll cover how to grow your audience, build a community, and yes, even monetize your podcast when the time is right. But remember: the journey to podcasting greatness starts with passion, not profit.

But Wait, There's More!

By now, I hope you're getting excited about the possibilities podcasting offers. Maybe you've already got a killer idea for a show, or maybe you're still brainstorming. Either way, you're in the right place. This book is going to guide you through every step of the process, from picking a podcast topic that lights you up, to figuring out which microphone won't make you sound like you're recording from the bottom of a well. We'll cover the basics of equipment, recording, and editing in a way that won't make your head explode (promise), and we'll dive into strategies for growing your audience and building a brand around your podcast. And if you're an experienced podcaster looking to scale and monetize, don't worry—I've got some advanced tricks up my sleeve for you, too.

The best part? You don't have to be an expert in any of this stuff yet. Seriously, nobody starts out knowing everything. (Well, except maybe that one guy who has a podcast on literally everything. But we're not talking about him.) The point is, that this book will help you avoid some of the pitfalls that trip up new podcasters and give you the confidence to get behind the mic.

So, What's the Catch?

Here's the thing: podcasting is easy to start, but it's not always easy to maintain. The real challenge isn't just getting that first episode out there (though that can feel like a mountain in itself). It's staying consistent, improving your craft, and keeping your audience engaged over time. That's why this book isn't just about the technical stuff. We're also going to talk about the mindset and habits that make successful podcasters.

But hey, don't sweat it. We're going to tackle all of this with a hefty dose of humor because let's face it—if we take ourselves too seriously, what's the point? I'm here to help you demystify the process, make it fun, and show you that podcasting is within your reach. You don't have to be a tech wizard or a professional radio host to pull it off. You just have to be willing to try, learn, and—most importantly—press record.

Your Podcasting Journey Starts Here

So, you're still with me, huh? Good! That means you're already ahead of the game. Whether you're a podcasting newbie or a seasoned host looking to take things to the next level, this book is designed for you. By the time we're done, you'll have everything you need to start your podcast with confidence—and maybe even have some fun along the way. Now, grab your microphone (or, you know, borrow one from a friend), because your podcasting journey is about to begin. Let's do this!

Part 1: Getting Started with Your Podcast Idea

Chapter 1: Choosing a Topic You Care About

Podcasting can feel like a massive undertaking when you're just starting out. There's equipment to buy, recording to do, editing to learn, and, of course, the looming question of "What on earth should my podcast even be about?" If that's where you're stuck, let's break it down together and make choosing a topic something that feels exciting and empowering, rather than overwhelming.

In this chapter, we're going to take it step by step, exploring how to pick a topic you genuinely care about, one that won't leave you feeling burned out after just a few episodes. We'll also look at how to balance your passion with what your potential audience wants to hear and dive into some practical exercises to help you discover your podcasting niche. Don't worry—by the end, you'll feel ready to tackle this decision and move forward with confidence.

1. Finding Your Passion: Why You Should Focus on a Subject That Excites You

Starting a podcast is easy. Sticking with it is the hard part. One of the most common reasons people stop podcasting after a few episodes is because they chose a topic they weren't really invested in. They went for what was trendy or what they *thought* would be popular, but it didn't hold their interest over time. To avoid that trap, the first thing you need to do is focus on something that excites you—something you could talk about for hours without getting bored.

Think about the things you love to talk about with friends or family. What are the topics that get you fired up, that make you lose track of time? Your podcast topic should come from a place of genuine curiosity or enthusiasm. If you pick a topic that bores you, it'll show in your episodes, and your listeners will pick up on that.

Why Passion Matters

Passion matters because podcasting is a long game. You're going to spend a lot of time researching, recording, and editing your episodes. If you're not excited about your subject, all of that work will feel like a chore—and when something feels like a chore, you're much more likely to give up on it. But when you're passionate about your topic, it won't feel like work. Sure, there will be hard days, but your love for the subject will keep you going.

Plus, passion is contagious. When you're genuinely excited about what you're talking about, your listeners will feel that excitement too. It'll make your show more engaging, more fun, and ultimately more successful.

How to Find Your Passion

If you're not sure what you're passionate about, don't stress. Sometimes our interests are so ingrained in our daily lives that we overlook them as potential podcast topics. Here are some prompts to help you think through what excites you:

- **What do you talk about the most?** Pay attention to the topics you bring up in conversation with friends and family. Do you love debating sports? Analyzing movies? Sharing stories about your travel adventures? Those could all be great podcast topics.

- **What could you spend hours reading or learning about?** If you find yourself constantly reading articles or watching videos on a particular subject, that's a good sign it could be a sustainable podcast topic. You'll be spending a lot of time researching your episodes, so it's important that you enjoy the process.

- **What would you do for free?** Think about the activities or hobbies you'd continue doing even if you weren't being paid for them. This can often point you toward a passion you'd love to talk about on a podcast.

2. Sustainability of Interest: Choosing a Topic That Won't Burn You Out

Even if you've found something you're passionate about, you need to consider how sustainable that passion will be over the long term. It's easy to get excited about an idea for a podcast, but will you still feel that same enthusiasm after you've done 10, 20, or 50 episodes? Choosing a topic that you can stick with is key to building a podcast that lasts.

Why Sustainability Is Important

Podcasting is a marathon, not a sprint. Many people start podcasts with high energy, but after a few episodes, they lose steam. That's often because they didn't think about whether their topic could sustain their interest (and their listeners' interest) over time.

When you choose a topic, it's important to consider how many episodes you could realistically produce. If your subject is too narrow, you might run out of things to talk about. On the other hand, if your topic is too broad or vague, you might struggle to keep your episodes focused and engaging.

How to Choose a Sustainable Topic

Here are some questions to ask yourself to ensure your podcast topic is sustainable:

- **Do I have enough to say about this?** Make a list of potential episode ideas for your podcast. If you can only come up with a handful of topics, you might run out of steam quickly. If, however, you find that the ideas keep flowing, that's a good sign you've chosen a sustainable topic.

- **Can this topic evolve?** Some of the best podcast topics are ones that allow for growth and evolution. For example, if your podcast is about a hobby or industry that's constantly changing (like technology, entertainment, or health), you'll never run out of fresh material. If your topic is more static, think about whether you can approach it from different angles over time.

- **Will I still care about this in a year?** Imagine yourself one year from now, still working on your podcast. Will you still be excited to talk about this subject? Or will you feel like you've said everything there is to say? It's important to choose a topic that has staying power.

3. Combining Passion with Audience Demand: Finding the Balance Between What You Love and What People Want to Hear

While it's important to choose a topic you're passionate about, it's also essential to think about your audience. After all, podcasting is about creating something that other people want to listen to. If your passion is too niche or too personal, you might struggle to attract listeners. But if you focus solely on what you think will be popular, you'll lose the joy that comes from talking about something you love.

The sweet spot is finding a balance between your passion and what your audience wants to hear.

Why Audience Demand Matters

Even the most passionate podcaster won't succeed if no one is listening. That's why it's important to consider what kind of content people are looking for. Are there existing podcasts in your chosen niche that have a loyal following? That's a good sign there's an audience for the topic. But you'll also want to make sure your podcast brings something new to the table.

How to Combine Passion and Demand

Here's how you can balance your passion with audience demand:

1. **Do Some Market Research**: Take some time to browse through the podcast charts in your genre. What are the top shows in your chosen niche? What kinds of episodes are they producing? What do their reviews say about why listeners love (or hate) them? This research can help you identify gaps in the market where your podcast can offer something different.

2. **Test Your Idea on Friends and Family**: Talk to people in your life who might be interested in your podcast topic. See if they find it as exciting as you do. Sometimes we think a subject is fascinating, but when we share it with others, we realize it might not be as universally appealing. Getting feedback early can help you refine your idea.

3. **Use Online Communities**: Platforms like Reddit, Quora, or Facebook groups are great for gauging interest in specific topics. Join groups related to your podcast idea and see what people are talking about. What questions

are they asking? What are they passionate about? This can give you insights into what potential listeners want from a podcast.

4. **Find Your Unique Angle**: Even if your topic is something lots of people are already podcasting about, you can still make it your own. Think about how you can combine your passion with a unique perspective. Maybe you approach the topic from a different cultural or generational lens. Maybe you blend two passions together (e.g., discussing technology through the lens of history). The key is to find an angle that feels fresh and different while still appealing to an existing audience.

Examples of Successful Podcasts That Balance Passion and Demand

- **Armchair Expert**: Dax Shepard's *Armchair Expert* is a great example of a podcast that combines passion with audience demand. Shepard loves having deep, meaningful conversations with interesting people, and it's clear he's passionate about it. But he's also tapped into a broader audience by interviewing celebrities and public figures, which drives listener interest.

- **How I Built This**: Host Guy Raz is clearly passionate about entrepreneurship and storytelling, and that passion shines through in *How I Built This*. But the podcast is also successful because it taps into the audience's demand for inspiring, behind-the-scenes stories of how successful companies were built.

Chapter 2:

What Makes a Podcast Work?

Podcasting is booming, and the number of shows available today is mind-boggling. With over 2 million podcasts in existence and counting, you may wonder: *How do I make my podcast stand out?* The simple answer is, you must ensure your podcast works. But what does that really mean? It means creating a podcast that captures attention, keeps listeners coming back, and ultimately turns casual listeners into devoted fans.

In this chapter, we'll break down the key elements that make a podcast work in a crowded, competitive market. We'll cover how to make your show original and different, the power of consistency, the art of audience engagement, and finally, we'll dive into some practical exercises to help you evaluate successful podcasts and apply their strategies to your own show.

1. Originality and Differentiation: Stand Out or Fade Away

Let's face it, originality is hard to come by in today's world. Almost every idea seems to have been done before. But here's the thing: originality in podcasting doesn't always mean doing something that's *never* been done. It often means doing something in a way that's uniquely *you*.

Why Originality Matters

The podcast landscape is overflowing with shows. Whether it's a true crime mystery, a pop culture recap, or a business advice series, listeners have options. In this sea of choices, how do they decide what to listen to? They're not just looking for any show that covers the topic they like—they're looking for one with a voice, style, or perspective that resonates with them.

Your goal is to carve out a space in the podcasting world that only *you* can fill. Originality will help you stand out, and standing out is the first step toward building a loyal audience. Consider this: If your podcast sounds exactly like five others, why should someone listen to you instead of them? You need to offer something that differentiates you from the rest.

How to Be Original

Originality doesn't mean you have to reinvent the wheel. In fact, most successful podcasts take familiar concepts but add their own twist. Here's how you can inject originality into your podcast:

1. **Your Personality**: The easiest way to be original is to *be yourself*. No one else can replicate your personality, your sense of humour, or your perspective. Lean into your quirks and unique experiences—let your true self come through in every episode. Your personality might be the key reason someone tunes into your podcast over another.

2. **Format and Structure**: While many podcasts use tried-and-true formats (interviews, storytelling, roundtable discussions), you can experiment with how you structure your show. Maybe you combine elements of different formats, or maybe you find a way to introduce a recurring, unique segment that becomes a signature of your podcast.

3. **Niche Content**: Narrowing your focus to a niche topic is one of the best ways to stand out. Sure, there are thousands of podcasts about movies, but what if yours focuses specifically on *independent* films made before

1990? Or maybe your show doesn't just cover entrepreneurship—it focuses on entrepreneurs who have failed multiple times before succeeding. The more specific your niche, the easier it is to attract a passionate audience that's underserved by the broader market.

Examples of Original Podcasts

- **My Favorite Murder**: There are hundreds of true crime podcasts, but *My Favorite Murder* stood out because it combined dark, grisly stories with humour. The hosts, Karen Kilgariff and Georgia Hardstark, share their fascination with true crime while injecting banter, personal anecdotes, and lots of laughter. The combination of these elements made the show feel fresh and different from more straightforward true crime podcasts.

- **The Daily**: News podcasts are common, but *The Daily* by The New York Times managed to differentiate itself with its concise, storytelling approach. Rather than bombarding listeners with a long list of headlines, it focuses on a single story each episode and breaks it down in a digestible, engaging way.

2. Consistency: Regular Releases Lead to Success

Originality may hook your listeners, but consistency keeps them coming back for more. One of the biggest reasons podcasts fail to build an audience is because they're inconsistent. If listeners never know when (or if) they'll get another episode, they'll lose interest and move on.

Why Consistency Matters

Humans are creatures of habit, and podcast listeners are no different. When they find a podcast they like, they want to build it into their routine—maybe they listen every Tuesday on their commute or every Sunday while doing chores. But if your podcast releases episodes sporadically, you'll disrupt that routine and risk losing loyal listeners.

Additionally, consistent releases help build anticipation. If your audience knows that a new episode is coming every Wednesday, they'll start looking forward to it. If they don't know when the next episode is coming, they won't feel that same sense of excitement.

Finally, consistency helps your podcast grow through word of mouth. Listeners are more likely to recommend your show to others if they know it's reliable. No one wants to recommend a podcast only to find out the episodes dried up weeks ago.

How to Stay Consistent

Staying consistent can be challenging, especially if podcasting isn't your full-time job (yet). Here are some strategies to help you stay on track:

1. **Set a Realistic Schedule**: Don't commit to more than you can handle. If producing a weekly episode feels like too much, start with bi-weekly or monthly releases. It's

better to release consistently every two weeks than to burn out trying to produce a weekly show.

2. **Batch Record**: One of the best ways to maintain consistency is to batch-record episodes. This means recording multiple episodes in one sitting and then scheduling them for release over time. That way, if life gets busy, you'll still have episodes ready to go.

3. **Create a Content Calendar**: Plan your episodes in advance so you're never scrambling for ideas at the last minute. A content calendar will help you stay organized and ensure you always know what's coming next.

4. **Stay Flexible but Committed**: Life happens, and sometimes you might miss an episode. That's okay! The key is to be transparent with your audience—if you know you'll be taking a break, let them know in advance. And always aim to get back on track as soon as possible.

Examples of Consistent Podcasts

- **Stuff You Should Know**: Since 2008, *Stuff You Should Know* has been releasing episodes like clockwork. The show's consistency is one of the reasons it has remained so popular for so long—it's a reliable part of listeners' routines.

- **The Joe Rogan Experience**: Love him or hate him, Joe Rogan has built one of the most popular podcasts in the world, partly because of his relentless consistency. With multiple episodes released every week, listeners know they'll always have fresh content to dive into.

3. Audience Engagement: Building Loyalty and Retention

Engaging with your audience isn't just a nice-to-have—it's crucial to building loyalty and retaining listeners. Podcasts aren't a one-way street; they're a conversation, even if your listeners aren't physically in the room with you. When you engage with your audience, you make them feel like they're part of something bigger than just passive consumption.

Why Audience Engagement Matters

Listeners who feel connected to you and your podcast are more likely to become long-term fans. They'll be more invested in your show, more likely to share it with others, and more likely to support you through things like merchandise or crowdfunding.

Additionally, audience engagement helps you improve your podcast. When listeners give feedback, ask questions, or share their thoughts, they provide valuable insights that can help you shape future episodes. They'll tell you what they love, what they don't, and what they want more of.

Ways to Engage Your Audience

Engaging with your audience doesn't have to be time-consuming or complicated. Here are a few simple strategies:

1. **Respond to Comments and Messages**: If listeners leave comments on your social media posts, respond to them! If they send you messages, take the time to reply.

Acknowledging your listeners shows that you value their input and helps build a stronger connection.

2. **Encourage Listener Feedback**: Ask your audience for feedback on specific episodes or topics they want you to cover. You can do this through social media polls, email newsletters, or even directly in your podcast. For example, you could end each episode by asking listeners to submit their thoughts or questions for the next one.

3. **Create a Listener Community**: Building a community around your podcast can take audience engagement to the next level. Consider creating a Facebook group, Discord server, or subreddit where listeners can interact with each other and with you. This fosters a sense of belonging and keeps your audience engaged between episodes.

4. **Incorporate Listener Content**: One of the most powerful ways to engage your audience is to incorporate their content into your show. For example, you could do a listener Q&A episode, feature listener-submitted stories or questions, or even invite listeners to be guests on your podcast.

Examples of Engaged Podcasts

- **Welcome to Night Vale**: This popular fiction podcast has built a massive, engaged fan base. The creators frequently interact with listeners on social media, and they even created a "listener-powered" weather segment where fans submit songs to be featured on the show.

- **The Adventure Zone**: Another fan-engaged podcast, *The Adventure Zone* regularly incorporates fan art, listener theories, and fan-submitted questions into the show. This interaction strengthens the connection between the hosts and their audience.

Part 2 Crafting Your Podcast Format and Voice

Chapter 3: Finding Your Voice

One of the most exciting parts of starting a podcast is that it allows you to share your voice—literally and figuratively—with the world. But what does it really mean to find your "podcast voice"? For many new podcasters, this can be a tricky concept to nail down. It's not just about how you sound on the mic; it's about the tone, personality, and style that define your podcast and set it apart from others. In this chapter, we'll explore what it means to develop your podcast voice, the balance between authenticity and character, how to build listener trust through your voice, and some practical exercises to help you refine your vocal delivery.

1. What Is a Podcast Voice?

Your podcast voice is the overall tone, style, and personality that listeners come to associate with your show. It's how you sound, yes, but also how you *present* yourself. Your voice conveys your mood, your attitude, and your level of engagement with the subject matter. It's a critical element of podcasting because it's what makes your podcast feel human and relatable. Without a strong voice, your podcast can feel flat or impersonal, making it harder to build an audience.

Defining Your Tone

The tone of your podcast is how you communicate emotionally with your listeners. Do you want your show to feel lighthearted and fun? Or maybe you're going for a more serious, intellectual tone. Your tone should align with your subject matter, but it also needs to reflect *you* as the host. For example, a podcast about mental health might have a calm, empathetic tone, while a sports podcast might be more energetic and fast-paced. Whatever tone you choose, consistency is key. Listeners will come to expect a certain style from you, and staying consistent helps them feel comfortable with your show.

Personality and Style

While tone sets the mood, your personality is what makes your podcast unique. It's the way you talk, the words you choose, your sense of humour (or lack thereof), and how you approach your subject matter. Your podcast should reflect your personality—don't feel like you need to conform to someone else's idea of what a "good podcaster" sounds like. Your style, meanwhile, is the combination of your personality, tone, and how you structure your show. Do you prefer a more conversational, laid-back style, or is your podcast more polished and scripted? Both approaches can work, but it's important to choose the one that feels most comfortable for you. When you find a style that matches your personality, your podcast will feel more authentic and enjoyable to produce.

2. Authenticity vs. Character: Being Yourself vs. Creating a Persona

One of the biggest debates in podcasting is whether you should be 100% authentic or create a character or persona to host your show. Both approaches can work, but it's important to understand the pros and cons of each and figure out what feels right for you.

Being Yourself

Many podcasters find that the easiest and most effective way to connect with their audience is by simply being themselves. Authenticity resonates with listeners—they can tell when a host is being genuine, and that builds trust. Being yourself on your podcast means letting your real personality shine through, including your quirks, your sense of humour, and even your vulnerabilities.

Being authentic doesn't mean you have to share every detail of your life or be overly personal. It just means speaking in your natural voice, expressing your true opinions, and not trying to force yourself into a mould that doesn't fit. The beauty of authenticity is that it allows you to build a podcast that's uniquely yours.

Creating a Persona

On the flip side, some podcasters choose to create a persona or character for their show. This can be especially useful if your podcast is more entertainment-based, or if you feel like your natural self doesn't fit the tone you're going for. Think of how some radio DJs or TV hosts develop a stage persona that's a bit different from their real personality.

Creating a persona can give you the freedom to experiment with a different version of yourself or even adopt a whole new character. It can be a fun way to explore topics with a fresh perspective, but it does come with challenges. Maintaining a persona over time can be exhausting, and it might make it harder to build an authentic connection with your listeners if they feel like they're not getting the "real" you.

The Middle Ground: Amplifying Yourself

One popular approach is to find a middle ground between authenticity and character. In this case, you're still being yourself, but you're amplifying certain aspects of your personality to fit the tone of your podcast. For example, you might play up your sense of humour or your enthusiasm when you're recording, even if you're a bit more low-key in real life. This strategy allows you to maintain authenticity while also giving your podcast a bit more energy or polish. It's about finding the right balance between being genuine and being entertaining.

3. Building Listener Trust and Connection

One of the biggest advantages of podcasting is that it's an intimate medium. When listeners put in their headphones and hear your voice in their ears, it creates a sense of connection. Your voice becomes a regular part of their lives, whether they're commuting, exercising, or just relaxing at home. Building listener trust through your voice is crucial for creating a loyal audience that keeps coming back for more.

Why Trust Matters

Trust is the foundation of any successful podcast. When listeners trust you, they're more likely to stick with your show, recommend it to others, and even support you financially (through things like Patreon or merchandise). But trust isn't built overnight—it's something you develop over time by being consistent, reliable, and transparent.

Your voice plays a huge role in building trust. If you sound confident, informed, and approachable, listeners will feel more comfortable trusting your opinions and insights. On the other hand, if your delivery feels stiff, robotic, or uncertain, it may be harder for listeners to connect with you.

How to Build Trust with Your Voice

Here are some tips for using your voice to build trust and connection with your audience:

- **Be Consistent**: Consistency in your tone, style, and release schedule helps build trust. When listeners know what to expect from you, they're more likely to feel comfortable and loyal to your show.

- **Be Honest**: Don't be afraid to admit when you don't know something or when you've made a mistake. Being upfront about your limitations or correcting errors in future episodes shows listeners that you're honest and trustworthy.

- **Use Empathy**: Speak to your audience as if you're having a conversation with a friend. Be mindful of their feelings, experiences, and perspectives, especially when discussing sensitive topics. Empathy in your voice makes your listeners feel heard and valued.

- **Show Enthusiasm**: Enthusiasm is contagious. If you're genuinely excited about what you're talking about, it will come through in your voice and make listeners excited too. Passion is one of the best ways to build a connection with your audience.

4. Voice Exercises: Techniques to Practice Clarity, Warmth, and Cadence

Finding your podcast voice isn't just about choosing the right tone or style—it's also about developing the physical qualities of your voice. Clarity, warmth, and cadence all contribute to how engaging and easy-to-listen-to your voice is. Luckily, there are practical exercises you can do to improve your vocal delivery.

Clarity

Clear speech is essential for podcasting. If listeners can't understand what you're saying, they'll quickly lose interest. Here are some exercises to help you improve clarity:

- **Articulation Drills**: Practice enunciating your words clearly by repeating tongue twisters or difficult-to-pronounce phrases. Start slow, then gradually increase your speed while maintaining clarity. Some classic examples include:
- "She sells seashells by the seashore."
- "Red leather, yellow leather."

- **Record and Review**: Record yourself speaking and play it back. Listen for any mumbled words or unclear phrases, and work on speaking more clearly in those areas.

Warmth

Warmth in your voice makes you sound approachable and relatable. It's especially important for building a connection with your audience. Here's how you can practice bringing warmth into your voice:

- **Smile While You Speak**: It may sound odd, but smiling while you talk can actually make your voice sound warmer and more inviting. Give it a try—record yourself speaking with and without a smile, and notice the difference.

- **Breath Control**: Warmth comes from a relaxed, controlled voice. Practice deep breathing exercises to calm your nerves and ensure that you're speaking from a place of ease. Inhale deeply through your nose, then exhale slowly through your mouth, making sure your breath is steady and even.

Cadence

Cadence refers to the rhythm and flow of your speech. Speaking too quickly can overwhelm listeners, while speaking too slowly can bore them. Finding a natural cadence will make your podcast more engaging and easier to follow.

- **Pacing Exercises**: Try reading a short paragraph out loud at different speeds—once very slowly, once very quickly, and then at a natural, conversational pace. This will help you become more aware of your pacing and find a rhythm that feels comfortable.

- **Pausing for Effect**: Don't be afraid to pause occasionally to emphasize a point or let an idea sink in. Pauses can add drama and keep your listeners engaged, so practice using them intentionally in your delivery.

Chapter 4: Deciding on a Format

One of the most important decisions you'll make when starting a podcast is choosing the right format for your show.

Your format will define the overall structure of your episodes, the style of storytelling or discussion, and how you engage with your audience. Whether you're drawn to narrative storytelling, interview-based shows, casual conversations with co-hosts, or the challenge of hosting solo, the format you choose will set the tone for your podcast.

In this chapter, we'll explore the four most common podcast formats—narrative, interview-based, conversational, and solo—and help you figure out which one might be the best fit for your personality and podcast theme. We'll also discuss some practical tips for testing out different formats before you commit to one.

1. Narrative Podcasts: Pros and Cons of Producing Scripted and Story-Driven Shows

Narrative podcasts are story-driven and often involve a scripted structure. These types of podcasts are like audio documentaries or serialized stories, where each episode builds on a cohesive narrative. They can focus on real-life events, historical topics, personal stories, or fictional tales.

Pros of Narrative Podcasts

- **Storytelling Power**: If you love storytelling, a narrative podcast can be an excellent way to showcase your creativity. The structure allows you to weave together different elements—interviews, sound effects, music, and narration—to create an immersive listening experience.

- **Engagement**: Listeners often get hooked on narrative podcasts because of their immersive and suspenseful nature. If you're telling a compelling story, people will want to tune in to see what happens next.

- **Cohesive Structure**: Since narrative podcasts are scripted, they tend to have a polished and professional feel. You can carefully plan and edit each episode to make sure the pacing is right and the story flows seamlessly.

Cons of Narrative Podcasts

- **Time-Consuming**: Writing, editing, and producing a scripted podcast can be very time-intensive. You'll need to do a lot of planning upfront, and each episode will likely require multiple rounds of revisions and fine-tuning.

- **High Production Demands**: Narrative podcasts often involve more complex production elements, such as sound effects, music scoring, and multi-track editing. If you're new to podcasting, this can be a steep learning curve.

- **Listener Commitment**: Narrative podcasts usually require listeners to follow along from the beginning, which means you may not attract as many casual listeners. People who find your show later might need to go back to earlier episodes to catch up.

Examples of Successful Narrative Podcasts

- *Serial*: The gold standard for narrative, true-crime podcasts, *Serial* hooked millions of listeners with its detailed storytelling and serialized format.
- *Welcome to Night Vale*: A fictional, scripted podcast that blends storytelling with surreal, comedic elements, set in a strange desert town.

2. Interview-Based Podcasts: Structuring Shows Around Guests

Interview-based podcasts are among the most popular formats. They typically feature a host (or hosts) who interview guests—whether they're experts, celebrities, or everyday people with interesting stories to tell. The focus is on exploring the guest's knowledge, experience, or unique perspective on a particular topic.

Pros of Interview-Based Podcasts

- **Variety**: Each guest brings new energy, insights, and topics to your podcast, which can keep the content fresh and interesting for your audience.

- **Easy to Scale**: Because the guest provides much of the content, interview-based podcasts can be easier to produce than fully scripted shows. The conversational nature often requires less writing and planning upfront.

- **Networking Opportunities**: Hosting interviews gives you the chance to connect with interesting people in your field, build relationships, and even grow your own influence through association with your guests.

Cons of Interview-Based Podcasts

- **Booking Challenges**: Securing high-quality guests can be difficult, especially when you're just starting out. It may take time to build credibility and attract guests who add value to your podcast.

- **Inconsistent Quality**: Not all guests are great at speaking or telling their stories in an engaging way. You may have to work hard as the host to guide the conversation and keep it interesting.

- **Repetitiveness**: Without careful planning, interview-based podcasts can become repetitive, especially if you're interviewing people on similar topics week after week. You'll need to think creatively to keep the content varied.

Tips for Booking and Interviewing Guests

- **Start Small**: If you're having trouble booking big-name guests, start with people in your local community or within your personal network. Once you've built a few episodes with solid interviews, it'll be easier to attract bigger guests.

- **Research Your Guests**: Before each interview, spend time researching your guests and the topics they're known for. Ask thoughtful questions that go beyond surface-level information. This shows your guest that you're prepared and will likely lead to a more in-depth conversation.

- **Let the Conversation Flow**: While it's important to prepare questions in advance, don't be afraid to deviate from your script if the conversation takes an interesting turn. Some of the best moments come from unexpected tangents.

Examples of Successful Interview-Based Podcasts

- *The Tim Ferriss Show*: Tim Ferriss interviews top performers from various fields, providing in-depth discussions on personal and professional growth.
- *Fresh Air*: Host Terry Gross is known for her thoughtful and probing interviews with authors, artists, and public figures.

3. Conversational Podcasts: Co-Hosting Casual Conversations

Conversational podcasts typically involve two or more co-hosts engaging in casual, often unscripted, discussions about a particular topic. These shows can feel like you're eavesdropping on a fun conversation between friends, which is part of the appeal for listeners.

Pros of Conversational Podcasts

- **Natural Flow**: If you have great chemistry with your co-host(s), conversational podcasts can feel effortless and engaging. The relaxed style can make listeners feel like they're part of the conversation.

- **Less Structured**: Unlike narrative or interview-based podcasts, conversational podcasts don't require a strict structure or script, which can make them easier to produce and less time-consuming.

- **Multiple Perspectives**: Having more than one host allows you to explore different viewpoints and ideas, which can make for a richer and more dynamic discussion.

Cons of Conversational Podcasts

- **Maintaining Focus**: Without a clear structure, it can be easy for conversational podcasts to veer off-topic or lose focus. This can make the episodes feel scattered or disorganized if not carefully managed.

- **Co-Host Compatibility**: Chemistry between co-hosts is key. If you and your co-host don't have a great rapport or struggle to keep the conversation flowing, the podcast can feel awkward or forced.

- **Editing Challenges**: Unscripted conversations often lead to more filler words, interruptions, and off-topic rambling. This can make the editing process more time-consuming if you want to clean up the final product.

Tips for Co-Hosting a Podcast

- **Choose the Right Co-Host**: Make sure your co-host complements your style and has a similar level of commitment to the podcast. If you have different energy levels or ideas about where the show is headed, it can lead to friction.

- **Set Ground Rules**: Even if your show is casual, it's important to establish some basic ground rules for conversation flow, turn-taking, and episode structure. This will help keep things on track.

- **Prep Some Topics**: While you don't need a full script, it's helpful to have a list of topics or questions to guide the conversation. This ensures you have a fallback if the discussion stalls.

Examples of Successful Conversational Podcasts

- *My Favorite Murder*: A popular true-crime podcast that combines casual conversation between the two co-hosts with stories of murder cases.

- *The Joe Rogan Experience*: Joe Rogan's podcast often features long, free-flowing conversations with a wide range of guests, blending interviews and casual chat.

4. Solo Podcasts: The Challenges and Rewards of Hosting Alone

In a solo podcast, you're the only voice on the show. This format allows you full creative control over your content and is perfect for podcasts where the host shares their expertise, opinions, or personal experiences. Solo podcasts are common in niches like education, self-improvement, or personal storytelling.

Pros of Solo Podcasts

- **Complete Control**: You have full autonomy over the content, pacing, and direction of the podcast. There's no need to rely on guests or co-hosts, which can simplify the production process.

- **Build Authority**: Solo podcasts can help you establish yourself as an authority in your niche. If you have valuable knowledge or expertise, a solo show is a great platform for sharing it with your audience.

- **Flexibility**: Without the need to coordinate with guests or co-hosts, you have more flexibility to record when and how you want.

Cons of Solo Podcasts

- **More Pressure**: Being the sole voice on your podcast means all the pressure is on you to keep things interesting. You'll need to be comfortable talking for extended periods without the support of a co-host or guest.

- **Monotony Risk**: Without other voices to break up the content, solo podcasts can risk feeling monotonous. You'll need to work hard to vary your delivery, tone, and pacing to keep listeners engaged.

- **Limited Interaction**: One of the downsides of solo podcasting is the lack of interaction. With no guests or co-hosts to bounce ideas off of, it can feel more like a monologue than a conversation.

Tips for Hosting a Solo Podcast

- **Script or Outline**: Even if you don't write out your entire episode, it's helpful to have a detailed outline or script to keep you on track. This ensures your solo episodes remain focused and don't meander.

- **Use Variety**: To avoid monotony, try mixing up your solo episodes with different formats. For example, you could alternate between educational episodes, personal stories, and Q&A sessions where you answer listener questions.

- **Engage with Your Audience**: Encourage your audience to interact with you by leaving comments, sending questions, or participating in polls. This can help you feel more connected to your listeners, even though you're recording alone.

Examples of Successful Solo Podcasts

- *The Dave Ramsey Show*: Dave Ramsey hosts a solo podcast where he provides financial advice and answers listener questions.

- *Dan Carlin's Hardcore History*: Dan Carlin's solo, long-form podcast takes deep dives into historical events with a storytelling approach.

5. Practical Tips: How to Test Formats and Find What Works for You

Choosing the right podcast format is an important decision, but it doesn't have to be set in stone. Here are a few practical tips for testing out different formats before you fully commit:

- **Try a Pilot Episode**: Record a pilot episode in each format you're considering (narrative, interview, conversational, solo) to see which one feels most natural for you. Don't be afraid to experiment.

- **Ask for Feedback**: Share your pilot episodes with friends, family, or a small group of listeners and ask for their honest feedback. Which format did they enjoy most? What felt engaging or awkward?

- **Consider Your Strengths**: Think about what you're naturally good at. Are you a strong storyteller? Do you enjoy having conversations with others? Are you comfortable speaking solo for long periods? Choose a format that plays to your strengths.

- **Start Simple**: If you're new to podcasting, start with a simpler format like conversational or solo podcasting. Once you gain confidence and experience, you can explore more complex formats like narrative storytelling.

Choosing the right format is a crucial step in creating a successful podcast. By understanding the pros and cons of different formats—narrative, interview, conversational, and solo—you can find the one that best fits your personality, podcast theme and production capacity. Remember, there's no one-size-fits-all approach to podcasting, and you can always experiment and evolve as you go!

Part 3 Equipment, Recording, and Editing

Chapter 5 Demystifying the Tech and Making It Fun

All right, folks, it's time to talk tech—but don't run away just yet! I know for many people, the thought of recording equipment, software, and editing feels like a terrifying plunge into a confusing world of wires, buttons, and sound waves. But fear not, dear reader, because I'm here to make this as painless as possible. In fact, I dare say you might even enjoy it! Think of this chapter as a guided tour through a museum of podcasting gear and techniques, except instead of a tour guide with a droning voice, you've got me—your friendly, sarcastic podcaster who promises to make you laugh while you learn.

Now, I'll admit that podcasting involves a bit of a learning curve, especially on the technical side. But don't worry, we'll take it step by step, and by the end of this chapter, you'll know exactly what gear you need, how to set it up, and how to record and edit your first episode like a pro. The best part? You don't need to take out a second mortgage to get started. Let's jump in.

1. Gear Recommendations: From Shoestring Budget to Mid-Level Magic

When you think of podcasting gear, you might imagine a glamorous recording studio with big, expensive microphones, fancy soundboards, and headphones that make you feel like you're at a private concert. And sure, if you've got the budget, you can build a studio that would make Joe Rogan jealous. But let's be real—most of us are starting with the basics. The good news is that podcasting doesn't require a million-dollar setup. In fact, you can get going with stuff you might already have lying around the house.

Let's look at three different gear setups based on your budget:

1.1 The Super-Budget Setup

You've got ambition, passion, and a killer podcast idea, but you don't have much cash. No problem! Here's what you can do:

- **Microphone:** Your microphone is your new best friend. This is where your podcast will shine—or flop. But let's be clear: you don't need a microphone that costs as much as a car to start out. Some of the biggest names in podcasting today began recording with the cheapest microphones they could find. If you're really strapped for cash, you can literally start by using the microphone on your smartphone or laptop. Yes, it's not going to give you studio-quality sound, but for Episode 1, it will do just fine. As far as actual microphones go, you can find decent USB mics for under $50, like the **Fifine K669B** or the classic **Blue Snowball iCE**. These mics plug right into your computer, and you're good to go. You'll sound better than you would using a phone mic, and they won't break the bank.

- **Pop Filter:** A pop filter is that round thing you see in front of microphones in studios. It softens those sharp "P" and "B" sounds (known as plosives). You can pick one up for about $10, or if you're feeling crafty, make your own with a wire hanger and some pantyhose (seriously, it works).

- **Headphones:** Even if you're on a budget, it's worth investing in a decent pair of closed-back headphones. Why closed-back? Because they don't leak sound into your microphone while you're recording. The **Sony MDR7506** headphones are a popular option among podcasters, and they're affordable.

- **Recording Software:** For zero dollars, you can't beat **Audacity**. It's free, easy to use, and works on both Windows and Mac. We'll talk more about how to use it later, but for now, just know that you don't need expensive software to edit your podcast.

1.2 The Sweet Spot Setup

If you've got a little more cash to spend, you can upgrade your gear without getting into the realm of professional-grade equipment.

- **Microphone:** The **Audio-Technica ATR2100x** is a versatile mic that works both as a USB mic and an XLR mic (which is a fancier connection type that we'll talk about in a bit). It offers a noticeable improvement in sound quality over the super-budget mics, and it's still affordable, usually around $100. If you're ready to invest a little more, the **Samson Q2U** is another excellent option that won't break the bank.

- **Audio Interface (Optional):** If you've moved beyond USB mics, you might want to step up to XLR mics. For that, you'll need an **audio interface**. Think of it as a middleman between your microphone and your computer. The **Focusrite Scarlett 2i2** is a popular choice because it's simple, reliable, and not too pricey. But this is totally optional at this stage—you can stick with USB if you're not ready for this.

- **Pop Filter, Boom Arm, and Headphones:** Same as the budget setup—pop filters and boom arms are cheap but make you look like a pro. Headphones like the **Audio-Technica ATH-M50x** are a great choice in this price range.

- **Recording Software:** You can still use Audacity, or if you've got a Mac, **GarageBand** is a great option that's free and comes pre-installed. It's a little more polished than Audacity, and you can easily add music and sound effects.

1.3 The Pro Podcaster Setup

Alright, you're serious about this. Maybe you've already got a few episodes under your belt, and now you're ready to upgrade to something more professional.

- **Microphone:** The **Shure SM7B** is the gold standard in podcasting mics. It's the same mic used by big-time podcasters, radio hosts, and even some musicians. This mic requires an XLR connection, so you'll need an audio interface, and it also benefits from a **Cloudlifter** or another kind of preamp to boost its signal. Yeah, it's pricey, but if you're all-in on podcasting, it's worth every penny.

- **Audio Interface:** The **Rodecaster Pro** is not just an interface—it's an all-in-one podcast production studio. It has everything you need to record multiple mics, mix audio, and even add sound effects in real time. It's expensive, but it's a dream for podcasters who want to take their show to the next level.

- **Other Gear:** At this point, you'll have all the basics—pop filter, boom arm, quality headphones, and maybe even some **soundproofing panels** to cut down on echo and noise in your recording space.

2. Recording Software: From Free to Fancy

Now that you've got your gear sorted, it's time to choose your recording software. This is where the magic happens—the software you use to record and edit your podcast. Don't worry, I'm not going to hit you with confusing jargon. Let's break it down.

2.1 Audacity (Free)

We've already mentioned Audacity, but let's give it a little more love. It works on both Windows and Mac, This software is free and open-source, which means there's a huge community of users who can help you if you get stuck. It's not the prettiest software, but it's functional and will do everything you need it to do: record, edit, cut, paste, and export your audio. Plus, you can add plugins for things like noise reduction and audio effects. It's a solid choice for beginners.

2.2 GarageBand (Free for Mac Users)

If you're a Mac user, you've probably seen GarageBand lurking in your applications folder. Don't ignore it! GarageBand is more intuitive than Audacity, and it has some cool built-in features like loops and sound effects that you can use in your podcast. The interface is slick, and if you've ever used any Apple product, you'll feel right at home. It's perfect for podcasters who want a bit more polish without spending any money.

2.3 Adobe Audition (Paid)

For those who want to go pro, **Adobe Audition** is the way to go. It's part of Adobe's Creative Cloud suite, so it's not cheap, but it's powerful. Audition lets you record and edit with incredible precision, offers advanced noise reduction tools, and allows for multi-track editing (so you can record interviews, music, and effects on separate tracks). It's overkill for beginners, but if you're ready to take your podcast to the next level, it's worth considering.

2.4 Other Paid Software

There are plenty of other options out there, from **Hindenburg Journalist** to **Reaper**, each with its own set of features. If you're starting to get serious about podcasting, it might be worth trying out a few different programs to see which one feels best for you. Many of these paid options offer free trials, so you can test them before committing.

3. Editing Basics: From Rough to Polished

Editing is where your podcast truly comes to life. It's like polishing a diamond—you're taking something good and making it great. But don't worry, you don't need to be a professional sound engineer to make your podcast sound professional. Here's the basic process:

3.1 Cut the Fluff

The first step in editing is cutting out anything that doesn't belong. Maybe you rambled a bit, or maybe you and your co-host went off on a tangent that doesn't fit with the theme of the episode. Or maybe you just had some awkward pauses or moments where you lost your train of thought. Cut those out. Editing is also about pacing. You want your podcast to have a natural flow, so don't be afraid to cut out unnecessary sections. But here's the thing: don't over-edit. You don't want to strip out everything that makes you human. It's okay to leave in a few "ums" and "uhs," as long as they don't become distracting. Your goal is to sound conversational, not robotic.

3.2 Remove Background Noise

Background noise happens. Whether it's a fan running in the background or a bit of hiss from your microphone, there's always going to be some ambient noise in your recording. Luckily, most recording software has built-in noise reduction tools. In Audacity, for example, you can select a section of your audio where it's just background noise (like at the beginning or end), and the software will help you reduce or remove it from the entire track.

Just don't go too crazy with noise reduction—you don't want to make your voice sound like it's coming from inside a tin can. A little noise is normal, and most listeners won't even notice it.

3.3 Add Music and Effects

Music and sound effects can give your podcast a little extra flair. Maybe you want a catchy intro theme or some background music for certain sections. Or maybe you want to add sound effects to enhance your storytelling. Most editing software will let you do this with ease. Just drag and drop the audio file into your project, adjust the volume so it doesn't overpower your voice, and you're good to go.

But here's the thing: don't overdo it. Music and effects are great, but your voice is the star of the show. Keep the extras subtle and in the background, where they belong.

3.4 Level Out the Audio

One of the most common mistakes beginners make is having inconsistent audio levels. Maybe you're super loud in one section and super quiet in another. Or maybe your intro music is way louder than your voice, and your listeners have to constantly adjust the volume. This is where **normalizing** or **levelling** comes in. Most DAWs have a tool for this—it ensures that all the audio in your podcast is at a consistent volume, making for a more pleasant listening experience.

3.5 Final Polish

Once you've cut out the fluff, removed the noise, added music, and leveled everything out, it's time for the final polish. Listen to your podcast all the way through to make sure it sounds natural and flows well. Make any final tweaks, then export your audio as an MP3 or WAV file, and voilà! You've got yourself a podcast episode.

4. Make It Fun, Not Frustrating

I get it—editing can be a slog, especially if you're new to it. But here's the thing: it doesn't have to be a miserable process. Editing is your chance to shape your podcast into exactly what you want it to be. Think of it like sculpting a piece of art. Sure, it takes time and patience, but the end result is something you can be proud of.

Plus, the more you edit, the faster you'll get. Eventually, what took you two hours will only take 30 minutes. So hang in there and enjoy the process. And if you ever get stuck, remember: YouTube is your friend. There are thousands of tutorials out there to help you figure out whatever editing issue you're facing.

5. Actionable Takeaways:

1. **Start small with gear.** You don't need the fanciest mic—focus on getting something that fits your budget and sounds good enough for where you are right now.

2. **Experiment with recording software.** Try out Audacity or GarageBand, and see which one you feel most comfortable with.

3. **Practice editing basics.** Cut out dead air, filler words, and anything that doesn't belong, but don't over-edit.

4. **Use noise reduction tools.** Background noise happens—learn to reduce it without making your audio sound weird.

5. **Add music and effects sparingly.** Music is great, but don't let it steal the show. Keep it subtle.

6. **Level your audio.** Make sure your podcast's volume is consistent from start to finish.

7. **Enjoy the process.** Editing can be tedious, but it's also your chance to perfect your podcast. Take your time and have fun with it!

Chapter 6 : The Art of Recording

So, you've brainstormed your podcast idea, settled on a format, and even chosen your equipment. You're ready to record your first episode! But where do you start? Recording your podcast can feel like stepping into the unknown, but with a little bit of preparation and knowledge, you'll soon realize it's not as intimidating as it seems. In this chapter, we'll walk you through the process of recording your first episode, share some tips to ensure great audio quality, and highlight common recording mistakes (so you can avoid them!).

1. Recording Your First Episode: A Step-by-Step Guide

The first time you hit that "record" button, it might feel like you're walking into a minefield of technical unknowns. But fear not—recording a podcast is a lot easier than you might think. Let's break it down into a step-by-step process:

Step 1: Prepare Your Recording Space

Before you even think about pressing record, it's important to set up your recording space. You don't need a professional studio to achieve great sound quality, but there are a few things you can do to ensure your environment is suitable for recording:

- **Find a quiet space**: Choose a room that's away from noisy areas like the kitchen, laundry room, or street-facing windows. Soundproofing isn't necessary, but try to minimize background noise as much as possible.

- **Reduce echo**: Bare walls can cause your voice to bounce, creating an echoey effect. To reduce this, add soft furnishings like curtains, rugs, or even hang up some blankets. The goal is to "deaden" the space so sound doesn't bounce around as much.

- **Test the acoustics**: Do a few test recordings in different parts of your room to find the best spot. Clap your hands or talk out loud and listen to how the sound reflects. You'll want a spot with minimal echo and noise.

Step 2: Set Up Your Equipment

Once your space is ready, it's time to set up your equipment. Assuming you're working with basic gear (such as a USB microphone and headphones), here's how to get everything connected and ready:

- **Plug in your microphone**: If you're using a USB mic, plug it directly into your computer. For XLR microphones, connect them to your audio interface, which should then be connected to your computer.

- **Position your microphone**: Place your mic about six to eight inches from your mouth to avoid picking up heavy breathing or distortion. Use a pop filter to reduce harsh "p" and "s" sounds. Angle the microphone slightly off-axis so you're not speaking directly into it.

- **Wear headphones**: Wearing closed-back headphones during recording allows you to monitor your voice in real-time. This helps you catch any issues (like crackling or background noise) before they become bigger problems.

Step 3: Set Up Your Recording Software

Open your preferred recording software (like Audacity, GarageBand, or Adobe Audition) and create a new project. Here's what to check before you hit "record":

- **Audio settings**: Make sure your microphone is selected as the input device and that your recording settings match the industry standard (44.1 kHz sample rate, 16-bit or 24-bit depth).

- **Test levels**: Do a test recording to check your audio levels. Your voice should fall between -12 dB and -6 dB. If your levels are too low, you'll get a lot of background noise. If they're too high, your audio will clip and distort.

- **Record in WAV format**: It's best to record your raw audio in WAV format (rather than MP3), as it retains higher quality for editing. You can export to MP3 later for publishing.

Step 4: Record Your Episode

Now, it's time to record! Press that big red button and start talking. Here are some tips for a smooth recording process:

- **Start with a script or outline**: You don't need to write out every word, but having a script or outline ensures you stay on track and don't forget key points.

- **Speak naturally**: Podcasting is all about connecting with your audience. Speak as if you're having a conversation with a friend—don't rush or feel like you need to sound overly formal.

- **Take breaks**: If you make a mistake, don't panic. Pause for a moment and start again. You can always edit out mistakes later.

- **Mark your mistakes**: Clap or make a loud noise if you mess up. This will create a spike in the audio waveform, making it easier to find the mistake during editing.

Step 5: Save Your Files

Once you've finished recording, make sure to save your audio file right away. Create a naming system that includes the episode number and date, so you can keep your files organized. For example: "Ep01_FirstRecording_2024.wav." Always back up your raw audio in multiple locations (like an external drive or cloud storage) to avoid losing your work.

2. Best Practices for Audio Quality

No matter how great your content is, poor audio quality can ruin the listener's experience. Luckily, there are several ways to ensure your podcast sounds clean and professional, even if you're recording at home.

1. Avoid Background Noise

Nothing distracts listeners faster than background noise—whether it's a barking dog, honking cars, or the hum of a refrigerator. Here's how to minimize unwanted sounds:

- **Use a quiet room**: As mentioned earlier, choose the quietest room in your house. Turn off any noisy appliances and inform others in your household when you're recording.

- **Consider a dynamic microphone**: If you're in a noisy environment, consider using a dynamic microphone (like the Shure SM58). These mics pick up less ambient noise than condenser microphones.

- **Noise gates**: In post-production, you can use a noise gate to automatically reduce background noise during silent parts of your recording.

2. Manage Echo and Reverb

Echo and reverb can make your podcast sound distant and unprofessional. To reduce these effects:

- **Record in a smaller, furnished room**: Large, empty rooms amplify reverb. Smaller spaces with plenty of soft materials (like carpets and curtains) will naturally absorb sound.

- **Soundproofing**: If you're serious about sound quality, consider investing in some basic soundproofing materials, such as acoustic foam panels or heavy drapes.

3. Prevent Pops and Sibilance

Pops (harsh "p" sounds) and sibilance (sharp "s" sounds) can be grating on the ears. To avoid these:

- **Use a pop filter**: A pop filter is a small screen placed in front of your microphone. It softens the force of your breath as you speak, reducing pops.

- **Speak slightly off-axis**: Position the microphone slightly to the side of your mouth (rather than directly in front). This reduces the intensity of plosive sounds.

4. Maintain Consistent Volume Levels

One common mistake among new podcasters is inconsistent volume levels. Your voice might be loud at the beginning and soft by the end, or you might have wild volume fluctuations throughout the episode. Here's how to keep things consistent:

- **Maintain a steady distance from the microphone**: Keep your mouth the same distance (6-8 inches) from the mic throughout the recording. Don't lean in or out too much as you speak.

- **Monitor with headphones**: Use headphones to monitor your volume in real-time. If you notice your voice getting too loud or too soft, adjust accordingly.

- **Use compression in editing**: Compression is an editing tool that evens out the volume of your recording, reducing the difference between loud and quiet parts.

3. Common Recording Mistakes (And How to Avoid Them)

Every podcaster makes mistakes—especially in the beginning. But the more you know upfront, the fewer issues you'll encounter. Here are some common mistakes and how to avoid them:

1. Over-Talking

It's easy to get excited and start talking over your co-host or guest. While this can happen in natural conversations, it becomes distracting in a podcast. Over-talking can also make editing a nightmare.

How to avoid it: Practice active listening. Wait for the other person to finish speaking before you respond. It's okay to have short pauses between speakers—these can be edited out later.

2. Poor Mic Technique

New podcasters often struggle with microphone technique. They might sit too far away from the mic, leading to quiet audio, or too close, causing distortion. They may also fidget, causing the mic to pick up unnecessary noise.

How to avoid it: Maintain a consistent distance (6-8 inches) from the mic. Use a mic stand to avoid holding or touching the microphone during recording.

3. Dead Air

Dead air refers to long pauses of silence where nothing is happening. While a pause here or there is fine, too much dead air can make your podcast sound awkward and unprofessional.

How to avoid it: If you lose your train of thought or need to take a break, mark the spot with a clap (for easy editing later) and then continue. You can edit out long pauses in post-production.

4. Speaking Too Fast or Too Slow

Your delivery speed plays a huge role in how engaging your podcast is. If you speak too fast, listeners may struggle to keep up. If you speak too slowly, they might get bored.

How to avoid it: Practice speaking at a moderate pace—neither too fast nor too slow. It helps to rehearse before recording, especially if you tend to speak quickly when nervous.

Recording your podcast is one of the most exciting steps in the podcasting process. By following these tips, you can ensure that your first recording session goes smoothly and that your audio quality is top-notch. Remember: it's okay to make mistakes—every podcaster has had their share of missteps. The key is to learn from them, improve your technique, and keep going.

Part 4 Promotion and Growth

Chapter 7: Your Podcast Deserves an Audience —Here's How to Get One

So, you've got a podcast episode (or a few) recorded, edited, and ready to roll. You've spent hours honing your voice, crafting your content, and making sure it sounds as polished as possible. Now what? Do you just toss it up on Apple Podcasts, cross your fingers, and hope millions of listeners stumble upon it like some kind of viral magic?

Not quite.

Growing a podcast audience doesn't happen by accident. It requires strategy, effort, and a little bit of elbow grease (don't worry, we'll supply the metaphorical elbow grease—you just focus on the strategy). But here's the good news: promoting and growing your podcast is not rocket science, nor does it have to cost a fortune. In fact, you can do most of it for free with a bit of savvy networking, social media know-how, and the right mindset.

In this chapter, we're going to cover everything you need to know about building your podcast audience—from your first listener to your loyal community of superfans. Whether you're just starting out or you're looking to scale your existing podcast, you'll find strategies here that will help you grow and engage with your audience in a meaningful way. Let's dive in.

1. The Importance of Niche: Know Thy Audience

Before we get into the nitty-gritty of promotion, let's talk about **niches**. Finding your niche is one of the most important things you can do as a podcaster, and yet it's often overlooked. If you're trying to appeal to *everyone*, you're actually appealing to *no one*. Harsh, I know, but it's true. Podcasts that try to be all things to all people end up lost in the shuffle because they don't stand out. On the other hand, podcasts with a clear niche—whether it's true crime, vegan cooking, or Dungeons & Dragons roleplaying—have a much better chance of attracting a loyal and engaged audience. So, the first step to promoting your podcast is to **define your niche**. Who is your podcast for? What topics are you covering? What makes you different from other podcasts in your genre? If you can answer these questions clearly, you'll have a much easier time promoting your show because you'll know *exactly* who you're talking to and where to find them.

2. The Basics: Make Sure Your Podcast Is Everywhere

Before you even start promoting, you need to make sure your podcast is available on all the major platforms. The more places people can find your show, the better. Here's a quick checklist of where you should be uploading your podcast:

- **Apple Podcasts** (formerly iTunes)

- **Spotify**

- **Google Podcasts**

- **Amazon Music** (Yes, they do podcasts now!)

- **Stitcher**

- **iHeartRadio**

- **Pandora**

- **TuneIn**

Most podcast hosting platforms (like Libsyn, Anchor, or Podbean) will distribute your podcast to these platforms automatically, but double-check to make sure your show is listed on all of them. You want to be everywhere your potential listeners are, so don't skip this step.

3. Social Media: Your Best Friend (And Sometimes Your Worst Enemy)

Now that your podcast is available everywhere, it's time to promote it. And where does most promotion happen in today's world? You guessed it—social media.

But here's the thing: **don't just shout into the void**. You can't just post "Hey, new episode is up!" once a week and expect to see a flood of listeners. Social media is a tool, not a magic wand. You need to engage with your audience in a way that makes them care about your content. Here's how you can use different platforms effectively:

3.1 Twitter: Short, Sweet, and Perfect for Podcasting

Twitter is like the town square of the internet—perfect for quick interactions, announcements, and sharing your latest episodes. Here are some tips for using Twitter to grow your podcast audience:

- **Engage with hashtags** relevant to your niche. For example, if you have a true crime podcast, use hashtags like #TrueCrimePodcast or #TrueCrimeCommunity. This will help people interested in your topic find your show.

- **Start conversations** with other podcasters or influencers in your niche. Don't just promote your podcast—ask questions, comment on other people's posts, and contribute to discussions. The more you engage with others, the more likely they are to check out your show.

- **Promote each episode** with a short, catchy tweet that includes a link to your podcast and relevant hashtags.

Include an intriguing quote from the episode or a question to hook potential listeners.

3.2 Instagram: Visual Storytelling for Your Podcast

Podcasts are audio, so how do you promote them on a visual platform like Instagram? It's all about **visual storytelling**. Here are a few strategies to make Instagram work for you:

- **Create audiograms**. An audiogram is a short video clip that features audio from your podcast with a visual soundwave or animation. You can use tools like Headliner or Wavve to create these for free. They're eye-catching and give people a taste of your podcast without requiring them to click away from Instagram.

- **Use Instagram Stories**. Stories are a great way to engage your audience with behind-the-scenes content, episode teasers, or polls related to your podcast topic. Plus, if you have over 10,000 followers, you can include a swipe-up link to your latest episode!

- **Post images or quotes** related to your podcast's topic. If you interview a guest, post a photo of them along with a notable quote from the episode. This gives people a reason to check out the full conversation.

- **Go live!** Instagram Live is a great way to interact with your audience in real-time. You can do a live Q&A about a recent episode or discuss upcoming episodes to build hype.

3.3 Facebook: The Old Reliable

While Facebook might not have the trendiness of TikTok or Instagram, it's still a powerful tool for promoting your podcast—especially if your audience skews a little older. Here's how to make Facebook work for you:

- **Create a Facebook Page** for your podcast. This gives you a hub where you can post new episodes, share related content, and interact with listeners.

- **Join Facebook groups** related to your niche. For example, if you have a podcast about vegan cooking, join vegan cooking groups and share your episodes there (as long as it's allowed by the group rules). Facebook groups are full of passionate, engaged people who could become loyal listeners.

- **Use Facebook ads**. If you've got a little budget to spend, Facebook ads can be highly targeted to reach the exact audience you want. You can run ads promoting your podcast to people who are already interested in similar topics.

3.4 TikTok: The New Kid on the Block

If your podcast's target audience is Gen Z or millennials, TikTok is where you need to be. This platform is all about **short, engaging videos**, so you'll need to get creative. Here are a few ideas:

- **Create behind-the-scenes videos** showing how you record your podcast, funny outtakes, or short clips from episodes.

- **Use trending sounds** or challenges. TikTok is all about trends, so find a way to tie your podcast into whatever's hot at the moment. You'd be surprised how creative you can get with this.

- **Collaborate with other TikTok creators**. If there are other creators in your niche, reach out to them for a collab. Maybe you can do a guest spot on each other's podcasts or create a TikTok challenge together.

3.5 LinkedIn: The Professional Option

If your podcast focuses on business, entrepreneurship, or professional development, LinkedIn might be the best place to promote it. Here's how:

- **Post articles or updates** about each episode. Give people a reason to listen by sharing insights or takeaways from your podcast.

- **Connect with industry leaders** and other professionals in your niche. The more you engage with their content, the more likely they are to check out your podcast.

4. Cross-Promotion: Help Each Other Grow

One of the best ways to grow your podcast audience is by collaborating with other podcasters. Cross-promotion allows you to tap into each other's audience and gain exposure to new listeners. Here's how to do it:

4.1 Guest Spots

Appearing as a guest on someone else's podcast is a fantastic way to get your name out there. When you're a guest, the host's audience gets to hear your voice, your ideas, and (hopefully) they'll want to check out your podcast afterward. Reach out to podcasters in your niche and offer to be a guest, and invite them to be guests on your show too. It's a win-win.

4.2 Promo Swaps

A promo swap is when you and another podcaster agree to promote each other's shows. For example, you could record a 30-second promo for their podcast, and they do the same for yours.

Part 5: Monetization

Chapter 8: How Podcasts Make Money

Podcasting can be a labour of love, but it doesn't have to be a passion project forever. Once you've built a dedicated audience, monetizing your podcast can become a viable and rewarding option, and while becoming a millionaire from podcasting is rare, many podcasters successfully generate a decent income by using a combination of sponsorships, listener support, merchandising, affiliate marketing, and other revenue streams.

This chapter will break down the main ways podcasts make money, with practical tips on how to get started, even if you don't yet have a massive audience. From finding and pitching sponsors to engaging with your most loyal listeners for support, you'll discover strategies that can turn your podcast into a revenue generator.

1. Sponsorships: How to Find and Pitch Sponsors

Sponsorships are one of the most popular ways to monetize a podcast. A sponsor pays you to mention their product or service during your podcast in exchange for exposure to your audience. However, finding and pitching sponsors, especially as a smaller podcast, can feel like a daunting task. Let's break it down.

1.1. When to Start Looking for Sponsors

The first question many podcasters ask is, "When am I ready to start pitching sponsors?" While you don't need to be Joe Rogan-level famous, sponsors typically look for podcasts with consistent listenership. That means having:

- **A loyal audience**: Even if your audience isn't huge, sponsors are interested in loyal and engaged listeners. If your audience regularly tunes in and trusts your recommendations, that's more valuable to sponsors than a larger, disinterested audience.

- **Steady download numbers**: Sponsors often prefer podcasts that receive at least 500-1,000 downloads per episode, but niche podcasts with smaller, more targeted audiences can still attract sponsorships.

1.2. How to Find Sponsors There are several ways to find sponsors, depending on your podcast's size, niche, and audience. Here's where to look:

- **Podcast networks**: Joining a podcast network can connect you with sponsors. These networks often have relationships with brands and help negotiate deals for their podcasters.

- **Ad marketplaces**: Platforms like Podcorn and AdvertiseCast allow you to list your podcast and connect with potential sponsors. You can browse opportunities and pitch directly to brands.

- **Direct outreach**: If there's a company you think would align well with your audience, don't hesitate to reach out directly. Many brands are open to sponsorships, especially in niche markets. Craft a compelling pitch that explains why their product would resonate with your listeners.

1.3. Structuring Sponsorship Deals

Once you've found a potential sponsor, the next step is to negotiate a deal. Sponsorships typically come in three main formats:

- **Pre-roll**: Ads that run at the beginning of the podcast, usually around 15-30 seconds.

- **Mid-roll**: Ads that run in the middle of the episode and are generally the most expensive, as they capture listeners' attention during the core content.

- **Post-roll**: Ads at the end of the episode. These are often less desirable because fewer listeners make it to the end of the episode.

CPM (Cost Per Mille): Most podcast ad deals are structured around CPM, which is the cost per 1,000 downloads or listens. For example, if you charge $20 CPM, and your episode gets 1,000 downloads, you'd earn $20 from that ad spot. CPM rates can vary based on your niche, audience engagement, and the sponsor's goals, typically ranging from $18-$50.

Flat fee: If you have a smaller but highly engaged audience, some sponsors may prefer a flat fee instead of CPM. This can be negotiated based on your specific audience and value proposition.

2. Listener Support Models: Platforms Like Patreon and Buy Me a Coffee

Not every podcast has the kind of audience size that attracts big sponsors right away, and that's okay. Listener support models allow you to monetize through direct contributions from your fans. This method can be especially effective if you have a loyal following who values your content and is willing to support your work financially.

2.1. Patreon

Patreon is one of the most popular platforms for listener support. It allows creators to set up membership tiers where fans can pledge a monthly amount in exchange for perks.

- **Setting up tiers**: The key to a successful Patreon is offering different levels of support with corresponding rewards. For example:
- $5/month: Access to exclusive behind-the-scenes content or bonus episodes.

- $10/month: Early access to episodes or the chance to vote on future content.

- $25/month: Personalized shoutouts on the podcast or exclusive merch.

- **Creating community**: Patreon isn't just about money—it's about building a community of super-fans who feel connected to your podcast. Engage with your patrons by offering polls, AMAs (Ask Me Anything sessions), and exclusive content to keep them invested in your show.

2.2. Buy Me a Coffee

If you don't want to commit to a membership model, **Buy Me a Coffee** is a more casual option. This platform allows fans to make one-time donations to support your podcast, with the option to "buy you a coffee" (or any other small amount).

- **No tiered system**: Unlike Patreon, Buy Me a Coffee doesn't require monthly pledges. Fans can simply make a one-time contribution whenever they feel like it.

- **Keep it simple**: This option works well for creators who don't want the pressure of constantly delivering exclusive content. It's great for accepting tips without having to commit to a subscription model.

2.3. Using Listener Support Effectively

While it's exciting to launch a Patreon or Buy Me a Coffee account, promoting these platforms effectively is crucial. Here's how to encourage your audience to support your work:

- **Mention it regularly**: Talk about your Patreon or Buy Me a Coffee page in your episodes. Don't overdo it, but make sure your listeners know where they can support you.

- **Make it personal**: Let your audience know how their support helps you create more content. Whether it's paying for hosting costs, equipment upgrades, or simply justifying the time spent on the podcast, people are more likely to donate when they understand the impact of their contribution.

3. Merchandising: Creating and Selling Podcast-Related Merchandise

Creating and selling merchandise is another fun and creative way to monetize your podcast. While it might not be your primary source of income, it can help you generate some extra cash and build a stronger connection with your audience.

3.1. What Kind of Merch Can You Create?

When it comes to podcast merch, the possibilities are endless. Here are a few ideas to get you started:

- **T-shirts and hoodies**: Clothing is a classic merch option. Create designs featuring your podcast's logo, memorable quotes, or inside jokes that your audience would appreciate.

- **Mugs**: Everyone loves a good mug, especially if it has a clever or funny message related to your podcast.

- **Stickers**: Stickers are a low-cost merch option that allows fans to rep your podcast on their laptops, water bottles, and more.

- **Posters and prints**: If you have a creative or visually striking podcast brand, you could offer posters or art prints as merch.

3.2. How to Sell Merch

The good news is that you don't need to buy and store a bunch of inventory to sell merch. Several platforms handle the production and shipping for you:

- **Print-on-demand services**: Platforms like TeeSpring, Redbubble, and Printful allow you to upload your designs, and they handle everything from production to shipping. You only pay for the products sold, making it a low-risk way to sell merch.

- **Shopify**: If you prefer more control over your merch store, you can set up a Shopify store and integrate it with print-on-demand services or manage your own inventory.

3.3. Promoting Your Merch

To sell your merch successfully, you'll need to promote it effectively:

- **Mention it on your podcast**: Give your merch a shout-out in your episodes. Let your listeners know where they can buy it and why they'll love it.

- **Offer exclusive designs**: Create limited-edition designs or offer exclusive merch for your most loyal listeners. This can create a sense of urgency and encourage your fans to buy.

4. Affiliate Marketing: How to Leverage Affiliate Links to Generate Revenue

Affiliate marketing is a great way to monetize your podcast by recommending products or services you genuinely believe in. Here's how it works: When you mention an affiliate product in your podcast and include a special link in your show notes, you earn a commission if your listeners make a purchase through that link.

4.1. How to Find Affiliate Programs

Many companies offer affiliate programs, but here are some common places to start:

- **Amazon Associates**: Amazon's affiliate program allows you to earn a small commission by recommending any product sold on Amazon. It's an easy way to monetize almost any podcast, as you can link to books, gear, or any product related to your content.

- **Niche affiliate programs**: Many niche companies offer affiliate programs. For example, if you run a podcast about fitness, you can find fitness equipment or supplement companies with affiliate programs. Just do a quick search for "(company name) affiliate program."

4.2. Promoting Affiliate Products

To succeed with affiliate marketing, authenticity is key. Don't just promote any product—promote products that you genuinely believe in and think your listeners will find valuable.

- **Integrate affiliate mentions naturally**: Avoid overloading your podcast with affiliate ads. Instead, mention the products organically in your conversation. For example, if you're talking about podcasting gear, you could recommend the microphone you use and include an affiliate link in the show notes.

- **Be transparent**: Let your listeners know that you're using affiliate links. It builds trust and ensures transparency. Plus, many countries have regulations requiring affiliate disclosures.

5. Practical Revenue Strategies: Monetizing Even a Small but Dedicated Audience

Finally, if you're wondering whether your small podcast can generate revenue, the answer is yes! You don't need a massive audience to start monetizing. Here are a few strategies to help you make money, even with a smaller listener base:

- **Leverage listener support**: As mentioned earlier, platforms like Patreon allow you to monetize a smaller, dedicated audience. Focus on building a community of loyal fans who are willing to support you financially.

- **Niche sponsorships**: Even if you don't have thousands of downloads, you can still find sponsors if your audience fits a specific niche. Companies targeting that niche may be willing to work with you, even if your numbers are smaller.

- **Experiment with different revenue streams**: Don't rely on just one way to monetize your podcast. Combine sponsorships, listener support, affiliate marketing, and merch sales to maximize your revenue potential.

Final Thoughts on Podcast Monetization

Monetizing a podcast isn't an overnight process, but it's achievable with the right strategies. Whether you're working with sponsors, listener support, or selling merch, there are plenty of ways to turn your passion into profit. Keep experimenting, stay authentic, and remember that success takes time. With patience and persistence, your podcast can grow into a sustainable source of income.

Chapter 9: Scaling Your Podcast

So, you've launched your podcast, built up a consistent listener base, and you're ready to take things to the next level. Scaling your podcast is an exciting step, but it can also feel like a daunting one. Growing your podcast from a small, dedicated audience into something bigger requires planning, strategy, and perhaps a few risks. But don't worry—it's completely within your reach.

In this chapter, we'll break down what scaling your podcast looks like, how to implement strategies to grow your audience, increase production quality, and explore new opportunities to expand your podcast's influence.

1. Understanding What It Means to Scale Your Podcast

Scaling your podcast isn't just about gaining more listeners (though that's certainly part of it). It's about improving all aspects of your podcast's production and reach, from the quality of your content to the marketing efforts that draw in new listeners. Here's what scaling typically involves:

- **Expanding your audience**: Reaching more listeners through promotion, collaborations, and other growth strategies.

- **Increasing episode frequency or length**: Adding more content or experimenting with longer episodes to offer more value to your audience.

- **Upgrading your production quality**: Improving audio quality, investing in better equipment, or even hiring a team to help with editing and production.

- **Exploring new platforms**: Expanding your presence across more listening platforms, social media channels, and video formats.

- **Diving into monetization**: Taking your monetization efforts up a notch with more sponsors, ads, listener support, or merchandise.

Scaling doesn't happen overnight, and it doesn't have to be perfect from the get-go. The goal is to gradually grow your podcast in a way that feels natural and sustainable to you.

2. Expanding Your Audience

The most obvious part of scaling your podcast is increasing your listener base. There are several ways to go about this, but here are a few key strategies to focus on:

2.1. Leveraging Social Media

Social media platforms are powerful tools for reaching new listeners and engaging with your existing audience. But simply posting about new episodes isn't enough. Here's how to make the most of social media:

- **Create platform-specific content**: Tailor your content to the platform. For example, use Instagram for behind-the-scenes content, Facebook for sharing episode links, and Twitter for quick updates or to join relevant conversations.

- **Engage with your followers**: Don't just post and disappear. Respond to comments, ask questions, run polls, and encourage conversations around your episodes.

- **Collaborate with influencers or other podcasters**: Work with social media influencers or fellow podcasters to cross-promote your podcast to a broader audience. Even small influencers in your niche can help bring in new listeners.

2.2. Using Paid Ads

While organic growth is ideal, paid ads can give your podcast the boost it needs. Consider investing in ads on platforms where your target audience spends the most time. Here are a few to explore:

- **Facebook and Instagram Ads**: You can run highly targeted ads based on demographics and interests. Make sure to include a clear call to action (CTA), like "Listen to our latest episode!"

- **Google Ads**: Promote your podcast episodes in search results or across YouTube if you've incorporated video content.

- **Spotify Ads**: If you're ready to put some money behind reaching listeners on the platform, Spotify's self-serve ad studio lets you create audio ads for your podcast that run on their free service.

2.3. Engaging Your Current Audience for Growth

Sometimes the best way to grow your audience is through your existing listeners. After all, word of mouth can be incredibly powerful. Encourage your audience to:

- **Share your episodes**: Ask them directly to share your podcast with friends or on social media. Offering incentives, such as giveaways or shout-outs, can boost participation.

- **Leave reviews and ratings**: Positive reviews on platforms like Apple Podcasts can help you climb the charts and reach new listeners. Don't be shy about reminding your audience to leave a review.

3. Increasing Production Quality

As your podcast grows, it's important that your production quality grows with it. Listeners may forgive some audio issues early on, but as your audience expands, expectations around sound quality and content delivery rise.

3.1. Investing in Better Equipment

If you've been using basic equipment, consider upgrading to more professional tools:

- **Microphones**: Upgrading to a higher-quality microphone can dramatically improve the clarity of your voice and eliminate background noise. Popular choices include the Shure SM7B or Audio-Technica AT2020.

- **Audio Interfaces and Mixers**: If you have a co-host or interview guests, a good audio interface (like Focusrite Scarlett) or mixer can help you manage multiple audio inputs with professional results.

- **Headphones and Pop Filters**: Better headphones help you catch more nuanced audio issues during editing, and a pop filter can eliminate unwanted "p" and "s" sounds while recording.

3.2. Improving Your Editing Skills

Even if you're not ready to hire an editor, learning some advanced audio editing techniques can make your podcast sound polished and professional. Spend time on:

- **Reducing background noise**: Tools like Audacity or Adobe Audition offer noise reduction features to clean up your recordings.

- **Mastering volume levels**: Ensure your audio levels are consistent throughout the episode to avoid peaks and dips that frustrate listeners.

- **Adding professional touches**: Incorporate subtle music or sound effects to enhance the listening experience without distracting from the content.

3.3. Hiring Help

If editing or producing your podcast is taking up too much time, consider hiring freelance help. You can find audio editors on platforms like Fiverr or Upwork, or even recruit a friend or colleague with the necessary skills.

4. Scaling Your Content

With a growing audience, there may be a demand for more frequent episodes or additional content beyond your standard episodes. Consider these strategies for scaling your content:

4.1. Increasing Episode Frequency

If you're currently releasing episodes weekly or bi-weekly, you may want to experiment with increasing your episode frequency to keep up with listener demand. However, don't sacrifice quality for quantity. Only increase frequency if you can maintain your production values and sustain your creative energy.

4.2. Offering Bonus or Exclusive Content

You don't have to release every new piece of content to your entire audience. Offering bonus or exclusive content to loyal listeners or subscribers can help maintain engagement and provide more value. Here's what you could offer:

- **Bonus episodes**: These could be extended interviews, behind-the-scenes content, or "lost" episodes that didn't make the regular feed.

- **Q&A sessions**: Let your listeners submit questions and dedicate an episode or segment to answering them.

- **Patreon exclusives**: If you're using a platform like Patreon, offer exclusive episodes or early access to regular content for your paying subscribers.

4.3. Expanding into New Formats

Consider experimenting with new formats to diversify your content. For instance, if you've primarily done solo episodes, you could try guest interviews or roundtable discussions. You could also explore video podcasts or live recordings to engage your audience in different ways.

5. Exploring New Opportunities for Growth

As your podcast scales, new opportunities for growth may present themselves. Here are some ways to expand your reach and brand:

5.1. Collaborating with Other Podcasters

Collaborations can open doors to new audiences and offer fresh perspectives for your listeners. Partner with podcasters who share a similar audience or topic but bring something new to the table. Consider:

- **Guest appearances**: Exchange guest spots on each other's shows.

- **Cross-promotions**: Feature each other's podcasts in intros or outros to expose your audience to new content.

- **Co-hosting special episodes**: Work together on a joint episode or mini-series that spans both of your shows.

5.2. Expanding Beyond Audio

Podcasts may start as audio projects, but many podcasters expand their brand into other formats. Here are a few ways to diversify:

- **Video podcasts**: Record your episodes on video and upload them to platforms like YouTube, where you can reach a broader audience.

- **Live shows**: As your audience grows, you may want to consider hosting live events or streaming your episodes in real time.

- **Books, courses, or webinars**: If your podcast has a specific niche, you could package your expertise into additional products, like eBooks or online courses.

6. Maintaining Consistency While Scaling

Finally, one of the key elements to scaling is consistency. As you grow, it can be tempting to overcommit and risk burnout. The key is to scale sustainably and maintain the level of consistency that got you this far.

- **Pace yourself**: Scaling doesn't have to happen all at once. It's better to gradually expand in a way that doesn't overwhelm you.

- **Stick to a schedule**: If you decide to increase your episode frequency, stick to a consistent release schedule so your audience knows when to expect new content.

- **Take breaks if needed**: Don't be afraid to take a break or introduce a seasonal format if you feel overextended. A brief pause with a well-communicated return date is better than burning out.

Chapter 10: It's time to Do It

So, here we are. You've made it to the end of this book about podcasting, and I have to say, I'm proud of you. I mean, you could've been doing a million other things right now. Maybe binge-watching your favorite show. Maybe learning how to bake sourdough bread, or perfecting your TikTok dance moves. But no. You're here, which means you're serious about starting your podcast—or at least curious enough to see this journey through. And that's a pretty big deal. But let's not get too sentimental. You didn't come here for a pat on the back; you came here to learn how to start a podcast. And by now, I hope you're feeling more confident, more prepared, and—dare I say it—excited to get behind that microphone and start talking. After all, we've covered everything from finding your voice and choosing a format, to editing your audio and promoting your show. You've got all the tools, strategies, and (hopefully) a few laughs along the way. So, what's left?

Well, now comes the hardest part. And no, it's not about mastering the technical side of things, or even figuring out how to monetize your podcast. It's about something much more daunting: actually *doing it*.

Taking the Leap

Here's the truth: the biggest obstacle standing between you and your podcast is you. I know it sounds harsh, but stay with me. Most people who want to start a podcast never do. Not because they can't, but because they overthink it. They worry about not being good enough, or not having the right equipment, or not knowing exactly what to say. They let fear of failure, or even fear of success, paralyze them.

And you know what? I get it. Starting something new is scary. Putting yourself out there—your voice, your ideas, your personality—for the world to hear can feel like jumping off a cliff. What if no one listens? What if people don't like it? What if it's all just a colossal waste of time?

But here's the thing: *What if it's not?*

What if people *do* listen? What if they love what you have to say, and you build a loyal audience who tunes in every week just to hear *you*? What if your podcast leads to opportunities you never even imagined—like collaborations, sponsorships, or even book deals? (Hey, it could happen!)

The point is, you'll never know unless you try. So if you take away one thing from this entire book, let it be this: **just start**. Don't wait until you have the perfect setup, or the perfect script, or the perfect idea. Spoiler alert: there's no such thing as perfect. Every podcaster you admire, every show you love—they all started from the same place: zero listeners, zero episodes, zero clue what they were doing. The difference is, they started anyway.

Perfection is the Enemy of Progress

Let's talk about perfectionism for a second, because it's one of the biggest creativity killers out there. You know that voice in your head that says, "It's not ready yet. I'll just tweak this one more thing. Maybe I'll record it again, just to be safe." Yeah, that voice is trying to sabotage you.

The reality is, that your first few episodes are not going to be perfect. They're just not. You'll fumble over your words, or forget to press record (been there, done that), or realise halfway through editing that your mic was too close to your mouth and now you sound like Darth Vader. It's going to happen. But guess what? That's okay. It's not about being perfect; it's about getting better with every episode. And the only way to get better is to *keep going*.

Think of your first episodes as a learning experience. Every podcaster has them. The awkward pauses, the overly scripted intros, the times when you thought you were hilarious but, in hindsight, maybe not so much. These are all part of the process. And the best part? Most listeners are incredibly forgiving—especially in the beginning. They know you're just starting out, and if they like you, they'll stick around as you find your groove.

So, embrace the imperfections. Own them. In fact, laugh about them. Podcasting is supposed to be fun, remember? And the more fun you're having, the more your listeners will enjoy the ride too.

Consistency is Key

Now, let's talk about another big hurdle for podcasters: consistency. Starting your podcast is one thing. Sticking with it? That's where the magic happens. A lot of new podcasters get through a handful of episodes before they hit what's known in the industry as "podfade." (Yep, it's a thing.) It's that point where life gets busy, or you run out of ideas, or you're just not feeling motivated anymore, so you stop recording. And then one missed episode turns into two, and before you know it, your podcast is gathering dust in the podcasting graveyard.

But here's the good news: you can avoid podfade by planning ahead. Remember how we talked about the importance of having a content calendar and a consistent release schedule? This is where that comes into play. When you know what you're going to talk about, and you've committed to a regular schedule—whether it's weekly, biweekly, or monthly—it keeps you accountable. It becomes part of your routine.

Of course, life happens, and sometimes you'll need to take a break. That's totally fine. But when you're consistent, not only do you build trust with your audience, but you also build momentum. The more episodes you put out, the more your listeners will look forward to your next one. And the more you create, the more confident you'll become.

Building Your Community

By now, you've probably realized that podcasting isn't just about talking into a microphone—it's about building a community. Your listeners aren't just numbers on a download report; they're real people who are choosing to spend their time with you. That's a big deal! So treat them like the valuable community they are.

As your podcast grows, take the time to engage with your audience. Respond to their comments and messages. Ask for their feedback. Encourage them to share their thoughts on social media or leave reviews. The more connected your listeners feel to you, the more likely they are to become loyal fans—and even advocates for your show.

And don't forget to nurture relationships with other podcasters, too. Collaborations, guest appearances, and cross-promotion can help you grow your audience and create valuable connections in the podcasting world. Podcasting is a collaborative medium, and the more you lift others up, the more you'll rise as well.

The Long Game

Let's be real: podcasting is a long game. Sure, some people hit it big with their very first episode, but for most of us, success doesn't happen overnight. It takes time to grow an audience, refine your style, and figure out what works. And that's okay.

The key is to keep going, even when it feels like you're shouting into the void. Even when your mom is the only one who's left a review (thanks, Mom). Even when you start questioning whether anyone is actually listening. Because here's the thing: if you're passionate about your podcast, that passion will shine through. And eventually, people will notice.

Podcasting is a marathon, not a sprint. It's about showing up, putting in the work, and trusting that the effort you put in today will pay off in the future. It's about learning, adapting, and growing. And most of all, it's about enjoying the process.

Final Words of Wisdom

Before we wrap up, let me leave you with a few final thoughts:

1. **Start small, but start.** You don't need the best equipment or the most polished concept to get started. All you need is the desire to share your voice.

2. **Embrace the learning curve.** You're going to make mistakes, and that's okay. Every episode is a chance to improve.

3. **Be consistent.** Whether you're releasing weekly or monthly, commit to a schedule that works for you and stick to it.

4. **Engage with your audience.** Your listeners are your biggest asset. Make them feel seen, heard, and appreciated.

5. **Keep going.** Podcasting is a long-term commitment, but the rewards—both personal and professional—are worth the effort.

At the end of the day, podcasting is about connection. It's about sharing your voice, your ideas, and your passions with the world. And the best part? There's room for everyone. Including you.

So go on. Press record. Let's see what you've got.